YOU'LL NEVER WALK ALONE

LIVERPOOL FOOTBALL CLUB

EST·1892

THE OFFICIAL
LIVERPOOL FC
ANNUAL 2017

Designed by Chris Dalrymple

A Grange Publication

ISBN 978-1-911287-08-7

CONTENTS

HONOURS LIST

League Champions
1900-01, 1905-06, 1921-22, 1922-23, 1946-47, 1963-64, 1965-66, 1972-73, 1975-76, 1976-77, 1978-79, 1979-80, 1981-82, 1982-83, 1983-84, 1985-86, 1987-88, 1989-90

European Cup Winners
1976-77, 1977-78, 1980-81, 1983-84, 2004-05

FA Cup Winners
1964-65, 1973-74, 1985-86, 1988-89, 1991-92, 2000-01, 2005-06

League Cup Winners
1980-81, 1981-82, 1982-83, 1983-84, 1994-95, 2000-01, 2002-03, 2011-12

UEFA Cup Winners
1972-73, 1975-76, 2000-01

European Super Cup Winners
1977, 2001, 2005

FA Charity Shield Winners
1964*, 1965*, 1966, 1974, 1976, 1977*, 1979, 1980, 1982, 1986*, 1988, 1989, 1990*, 2001, 2006
*shared

Super Cup Winners
1985-86

Division Two Winners
1893-94, 1895-96, 1904-05, 1961-62

Lancashire League Winners
1892-93

Reserve Division One Winners
1956-57, 1968-69, 1969-70, 1970-71, 1972-73, 1973-74, 1974-75, 1975-76, 1976-77, 1978-79, 1979-80, 1980-81, 1981-82, 1983-84, 1984-85, 1989-90, 1999-2000, 2007-08

FA Youth Cup Winners
1995-96, 2005-06, 2006-07

KLOPP OF THE KOP

Jürgen Klopp's managerial reign at Liverpool may still be in its infancy but the popular German has already made a big impression at the club. He arrived in October 2015 and proved an instant hit with players and supporters, leading the Reds to two major cup finals and offering genuine hope of a brighter, trophy-winning future.

This is the story of Klopp's first season at the Anfield helm, in his own words

Being unveiled as Liverpool manager…
"It's the biggest honour to be at one of the biggest clubs in this world. I'm looking forward to the intensity of football and how the people live football in Liverpool. It's a special club."

Being compared with Jose Mourinho (the so-called 'special one')…
"I'm a normal guy from the Black Forest. My mother is very proud. I

The legend of Anfield…
"I'm not a dreamer but I'm a romantic. I love the stories and Anfield is one of the best places in the football world."

Message to Liverpool supporters…
"I ask that you believe in this team and believe that together we can achieve great things."

His first game as Liverpool manager – a goalless draw at Spurs…
"The nil on the right side (conceded) is OK, for sure. On the other side, a nil (scored) doesn't give the same feeling! Football can be spectacular without goals, but our target is to keep clean sheets while scoring goals."

How Everton supporters reacted to his appointment as Liverpool manager…
"I've met some Evertonians in the street and they've been friendly. I've had taxi drivers who have been Everton fans. They've been really nice. At the beginning I thought 'okay, maybe they're happy I'm here because they think that means Liverpool won't have any success for the next 20 years!'"

After his team's impressive 4-1 victory over Manchester City at the Etihad…
"The best word I can say to describe

When things go wrong…

"We had a good plan in the first half but conceded two goals, so you can throw your plan in the purple bin."

Saluting the Kop with his players after they snatched a late draw at home draw to West Brom…

"I don't care what anyone outside Liverpool FC and our fans made of this, and I also don't care if I am mocked personally for what happened. It was a moment, and I am someone who reacts in the moment. But that moment was all about us: LFC."

Instilling a team ethic…

"I never want players who are 'happy' not to be playing – this is absolutely not allowed. However, it is important to have players who realise the team performance and team result comes ahead of everything else."

Losing the Capital One Cup final to Manchester City…

"We can change nothing now, but we can change something tomorrow morning. We will go on, we will get better. Today, we have to go the hard way. But we can see that if we carry on working really hard then there is light at the end of the tunnel. That's important."

Speaking ahead of the Europa League tie at Old Trafford…

"Hopefully it's a good atmosphere. I like it, even when everyone hates you. We will decide how good the atmosphere here is with our performance."

On laying down the law…

"I am not the guy who is going to go out and shout 'we are going to conquer the world' or something like this. But we will conquer the ball."

On Dejan Lovren's dramatic late winner in the Europa League quarter-final v Borussia Dortmund…

"I've had a lot of games in my life and not too many like this. If you read it in a book you think 'oh nice but it is really rare.'"

What goes through his mind when considering whether to sign a player…

"If I spoke to a player now and he told me: 'If you were playing in the Champions League next year then I would be really interested,' I would put the phone down. That is what I would say to players. It is about pushing the train, not jumping on a running train."

Liverpool's Europa League final defeat to Sevilla in Basel…

"We will come back stronger 100 per cent. It's not about the size of the squad or how many players we have, it's about using the time for training to get better, using this experience tonight and I promise everyone, we will use it. We will use it."

Klopp Profile

Full name: Jürgen Norbert Klopp
Born: Stuttgart, Germany
Date of Birth: 16 June 1967
Playing career:
FSV Mainz 05
(1990-2001)
Position: Striker/Defender
Managerial career:
FSV Mainz 05
(2001-2008),
Borussia Dortmund
(2008-15)
Major honours won:
Bundesliga
(2010/11 & 2011/12),
DFB Pokal
(2012)

GOALS GOALS GOALS
LIVERPOOL'S TOP 10 OF 2015/16

Headers, volleys, long-range pile-drivers, simple tap ins, stunning individual strikes and well worked team goals – even own goals... Liverpool scored a total of 98 goals during the 2015/16 season but what were the best? Here's a countdown of the top 10...

10. Martin Skrtel v Manchester City (a), FA Barclays Premier League, 21 November 2015

With the game nearing its conclusion, Skrtel emphatically ended any hopes of a City comeback with a thunderous half-volley. A corner from the right wasn't cleared and from the edge of the box the Slovakian defender powered his right foot through the ball, steering it through a crowded area and past a helpless Joe Hart.

9. Adam Lallana v Newcastle United (h), FA Barclays Premier League, 23 April 2016

Moreno's ball in from the left found Lallana ideally placed on the edge of the box. There was a line of Newcastle defenders ahead of him but that didn't deter the England midfielder who proceeded to curl a perfectly placed shot into the top corner of the Kop goal.

8. Daniel Sturridge v Aston Villa (h), FA Barclays Premier League, 26 September 2015

Sturridge temporarily eased the mounting pressure on boss Brendan Rodgers with two goals at home to Villa, the pick of which was this, his first of the season. Racing onto Milner's lofted ball over the top of the defence, he arrowed a well-executed left-footed volley low into the far corner of the Kop net.

7. Philippe Coutinho v Chelsea (a), FA Barclays Premier League, 31 October 2015

Receiving the ball 20 yards from goal, Coutinho sold Ramires a dummy and cut inside to a more central position on the edge of the box before dispatching a perfectly placed left-footed curler beyond the reach of Asmir Begović. It levelled the score on the stroke of half-time and set the Reds up for a memorable win.

6. Roberto Firmino v Manchester City (a), FA Barclays Premier League, 21 November 2015

Firmino's first goal in a red shirt was a simple effort but one that owed a lot to some glorious build-up play from his team-mates. A magnificent counter-attack from deep saw the ball worked to Can 25 yards out and his audacious backheel played in Coutinho who squared for his compatriot to tap home with ease from close-range.

5. Daniel Sturridge v Sevilla (Basel), Europa League final, 18 May 2016

Collecting the ball on the left edge of the box, Sturridge took a couple of touches and when a gap opened up between two defenders he seized the opportunity to sublimely steer a shot, with the outside of his right boot, beyond the outstretched arms of the goalkeeper and into the far corner.

4. Philippe Coutinho v Manchester United (a), Europa League, 17 March 2016

Just when United thought they were back in the tie, Coutinho scampered down the left wing to chase a Can through-ball, cut inside and advanced menacingly into the box, easily skipping past one defender before cheekily dinking the ball past David De Gea at the near post.

2. Philippe Coutinho v Stoke City (a), FA Barclays Premier League, 9 August 2015

Just four minutes remained of the season opener and a stalemate seemed inevitable until the little Brazilian spun off his marker then unleashed a glorious long-range effort that dipped and moved through the air before whistling past the outstretched Jack Butland to dramatically claim the points.

3. Roberto Firmino v Arsenal (h), FA Barclays Premier League, 13 January 2016

The Arsenal defenders could only look on in awe and the keeper had no chance as Liverpool restored their lead in this topsy-turvy game. From a central position 20 yards out, Firmino took one touch to control Milner's pass, steadied himself, looked up and nonchalantly curled the ball into the top corner of the net with pinpoint precision.

1. Christian Benteke v Manchester United (a), FA Barclays Premier League, 12 September 2015

Although it ultimately proved to be nothing more than a consolation strike, this goal will forever rank among the most spectacular ever scored by a Liverpool player at Old Trafford. Ibe crossed from the right and United's attempted clearance fell to Benteke who, with his back to goal, acrobatically netted with a stunning scissor-kick.

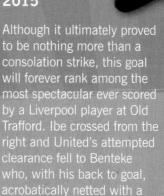

Liverpool's goalscorers 2015/16

Player	PL	LC	FA	EL	TOTAL
Daniel Sturridge	8	2	0	3	13
Philippe Coutinho	8	1	1	2	12
Roberto Firmino	10	0	0	1	11
Christian Benteke	9	0	0	1	10
Divock Origi	5	3	0	2	10
James Milner	5	0	0	2	7
Adam Lallana	4	0	0	3	7
Jordon Ibe	1	2	0	1	4
Joe Allen	2	0	1	0	3
Danny Ings	2	1	0	0	3
Nathaniel Clyne	1	1	0	0	2
Mamadou Sakho	1	0	0	1	2
Jordan Henderson	2	0	0	0	2
Own goals	1	0	0	1	2
Emre Can	1	0	0	1	2
Martin Skrtel	1	0	0	0	1
Jerome Sinclair	0	0	1	0	1
Kolo Touré	1	0	0	0	1
Brad Smith	0	0	1	0	1
João Carlos Teixeira	0	0	1	0	1
Dejan Lovren	0	0	0	1	1
Alberto Moreno	1	0	0	0	1
Sheyi Ojo	0	0	1	0	1

2015/16 goal stats, facts & figures

Breakdown of goals scored per competition:
Premier League - 63
League Cup - 10
FA Cup - 6
Europa League - 19

Average goals per game:
League 1.74 Overall 1.68

Minutes the goals were scored:
1 to 15: 11
16 to 30: 15
31 to 45: 20
56 to 60: 12
61 to 75: 22
76 to 90: 18
91 to 120: 0

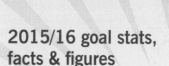

NEW MAIN STAND FACTS & FIGURES...

- 1.8 million bricks and blocks (6,000 tonnes of masonry) were used to expand the Main Stand at Anfield

- If all the bricks and blocks were used to create a 0.5m wall, it would stretch 40 miles, this is further than the length of the Channel Tunnel

- More than 5,000 tonnes of steel were used to expand the Main Stand, more than double the amount in the Blackpool Tower

- If every seat in the Main Stand was placed end to end it would stretch 6 miles, this is further than the distance from Anfield Stadium to the City Centre and back

- If all the surfaces that will need painting in the Main Stand were laid flat, this would create enough space to park 5,200 cars

- 760 panes of glass have been fitted in the Main Stand

- Each pane, if placed end to end would stretch 423m - this is around 4x further than the length of the Anfield pitch

- The main section of glass is 23m in height – this is taller than the Anfield Road Stand

- The combined internal floor spaces within the Main Stand are 5 times larger than the pitch

- The size of Anfield's truss meant that it took the UK's largest cranes over 12 hours to raise it into position above the Main Stand. Having a truss of this size means that there are no support pillars restricting views of the pitch

- The new Main Stand is one of the largest all-seater single stands in European football incorporating an additional 8,500 seats. The design will ensure that the unrivalled atmosphere and spirit of Anfield is retained, whilst taking the full stadium capacity to 54,000

Anfield redevelopment timeline...

4 December 2014: LFC confirms the redevelopment of Anfield Stadium

5 January 2015: Construction work gets underway

9 March 2015: The first steel is assembled at Anfield as work begins to erect the new structure behind the exisiting Main Stand

26 May 2015: Demolition of the 1970s structure behind the existing Main Stand begins

5 June 2015: The assembly of the Main Stand's new truss begins on site

1 July 2015: The Main Stand's first 28m high tower is erected between the Kop and the existing Stand

24 July 2015: Historic milestone at Anfield as the Main Stand's 650 tonne steel truss is lifted into place above the Stadium

3 September 2015: The first section of concrete terracing is installed to the new upper tier

4 September 2015: First bricks are laid on the Main Stand's new podium level which will eventually provide access into the Stand

8 September 2015: The first connection between the existing Main Stand and new steel structure is installed

2 November 2015: The first 70 tonne rear roof rafter is installed beneath the truss

4 January 2016: The upper tier concrete terrace is complete

25 January 2016: First glass installed in the Main Stand

11 February 2016: A host of Liverpool FC legends join construction workers on site for the Main Stand 'Topping Out' ceremony

3 March 2016: First front cantilever is installed above the Main Stand

4 April 2016: Last front cantilever is installed above the Main Stand

16 April 2016: 650 tonne crawler crane leaves Anfield as the main structure is complete

21 April 2016: First turnstile is installed to the Level 2 Podium

3 May 2016: First seat is installed to the new upper tier

12 May 2016: Work begins inside Anfield to expand the Main Stand after the last home game of the season

16 May 2016: Construction work begins inside the stadium to remove the existing roof

31 May 2016: Existing Main Stand roof is removed

15 June 2016: The Main Stand's new middle tier is complete

24 June 2016: First seats installed to the new lower tier

11 July 2016: Work gets underway to install the first of two giant crests to the front of the Main Stand

10 September 2016: Liverpool play in front of the new Main Stand for the first time

JUSTICE FOR THE 96

On 26 April 2016, after more than two years of proceedings, a jury concluded that the 96 Liverpool supporters who lost their lives at the Hillsborough disaster in 1989 had been unlawfully killed.

It was a momentous day in what had been a tireless 27-year long fight for justice by families of the victims, survivors and fellow supporters.

The inquest verdicts were greeted with a huge outpouring of emotion and the following evening a vigil took place on the steps of St George's Hall in Liverpool city centre, attended by a crowd of over 30,000.

The truth is finally out there but the terrible events that unfolded on that fateful day in Sheffield on 15 April 1989 will never be forgotten and the 96 men, women and children who didn't return home will forever be in our thoughts…

John Alfred Anderson (62)
Colin Mark Ashcroft (19)
James Gary Aspinall (18)
Kester Roger Marcus Ball (16)
Gerard Baron Snr (67)
Simon Bell (17)
Barry Sidney Bennett (26)
David John Benson (22)
David William Birtle (22)
Tony Bland (22)
Paul David Brady (21)
Andrew Mark Brookes (26)
Carl Brown (18)
David Steven Brown (25)
Henry Thomas Burke (47)
Peter Andrew Burkett (24)
Paul William Carlile (19)
Raymond Thomas Chapman (50)
Gary Christopher Church (19)
Joseph Clark (29)
Paul Clark (18)
Gary Collins (22)
Stephen Paul Copoc (20)
Tracey Elizabeth Cox (23)
James Philip Delaney (19)
Christopher Barry Devonside (18)
Christopher Edwards (29)
Vincent Michael Fitzsimmons (34)
Thomas Steven Fox (21)
Jon-Paul Gilhooley (10)
Barry Glover (27)
Ian Thomas Glover (20)
Derrick George Godwin (24)

Roy Harry Hamilton (34)
Philip Hammond (14)
Eric Hankin (33)
Gary Harrison (27)
Stephen Francis Harrison (31)
Peter Andrew Harrison (15)
David Hawley (39)
James Robert Hennessy (29)
Paul Anthony Hewitson (26)
Carl Darren Hewitt (17)
Nicholas Michael Hewitt (16)
Sarah Louise Hicks (19)
Victoria Jane Hicks (15)
Gordon Rodney Horn (20)
Arthur Horrocks (41)
Thomas Howard (39)
Thomas Anthony Howard (14)
Eric George Hughes (42)
Alan Johnston (29)
Christine Anne Jones (27)
Gary Philip Jones (18)
Richard Jones (25)
Nicholas Peter Joynes (27)
Anthony Peter Kelly (29)
Michael David Kelly (38)
Carl David Lewis (18)
David William Mather (19)
Brian Christopher Matthews (38)
Francis Joseph McAllister (27)
John McBrien (18)
Marian Hazel McCabe (21)
Joseph Daniel McCarthy (21)
Peter McDonnell (21)

Alan McGlone (28)
Keith McGrath (17)
Paul Brian Murray (14)
Lee Nicol (14)
Stephen Francis O'Neill (17)
Jonathon Owens (18)
William Roy Pemberton (23)
Carl William Rimmer (21)
David George Rimmer (38)
Graham John Roberts (24)
Steven Joseph Robinson (17)
Henry Charles Rogers (17)
Colin Andrew Hugh William Sefton (23)
Inger Shah (38)
Paula Ann Smith (26)
Adam Edward Spearritt (14)
Philip John Steele (15)
David Leonard Thomas (23)
Patrick John Thompson (35)
Peter Reuben Thompson (30)
Stuart Paul William Thompson (17)
Peter Francis Tootle (21)
Christopher James Traynor (26)
Martin Kevin Traynor (16)
Kevin Tyrrell (15)
Colin Wafer (19)
Ian David Whelan (19)
Martin Kenneth Wild (29)
Kevin Daniel Williams (15)
Graham John Wright (17)

Rest in Peace

PREMIER LEAGUE
HIGH FIVES

The 2015/16 Premier League campaign was far from a vintage one for Liverpool and its supporters. A final finishing position of 8th was disappointing but, in what was a season of major transition at Anfield, there were still more than a few moments to savour. Here are five of the finest...

Chelsea – 3-1
Stamford Bridge
Saturday 31 October 2015

Jürgen Klopp's reign as Liverpool manager was still in its infancy when the Reds travelled to the home of reigning champions Chelsea. The hosts had made a poor start to the season but were lifted by an early Ramires goal. However, Coutinho sparked an impressive comeback with an equalising goal deep in first half stoppage time. The little Brazilian added a second with 16 minutes remaining, while Benteke came off the bench to complete a memorable victory, Klopp's first in the Premier League.

Norwich City – 5-4
Carrow Road
Saturday 23 January 2016

Liverpool edged this nine-goal thriller in the most dramatic fashion. First they relinquished a 1-0 lead then fought back from 3-1 down to lead 4-3. Two minutes into injury time Norwich equalised and it looked as though the points would have to be shared. However, there was to be one final twist. With virtually the last kick of the game substitute Lallana struck the winner, sparking wild scenes of celebration and Klopp's glasses were broken amid the madness.

Manchester City – 4-1
Etihad Stadium
Saturday 21 November 2015

Liverpool turned on the style to blow title-chasing City out of the water inside a scintillating 32 minutes. The high-pressing game favoured by Klopp was clearly evident as the Reds tore into their shell-shocked opponents from almost the first whistle. Mangala put through his own net to open the scoring and the Reds were threatening to run riot when Coutinho and Firmino made it 3-0. Aguero managed to pull a goal back but the visitors' dominance was restored through a fourth goal by Skrtel late on.

14

Aston Villa – 6-0
Villa Park
Sunday 14 February 2016

Aston Villa may have been a side doomed for relegation but to score six goals without reply away from home is always a feat worthy of recognition. Once Sturridge opened the floodgates the result was never in doubt and Liverpool were ruthless in their execution, with six different scorers getting on the scoresheet. Milner added a second before the break then Can, Origi and Clyne all struck within seven minutes midway through the second half before Touré headed home the sixth to seal Liverpool's biggest win of the season.

Everton – 4-0
Anfield
Wednesday 20 April 2016

In what was undoubtedly the most one-sided Merseyside derby of the modern era Liverpool cruised to victory in emphatic fashion and left Everton thankful that the margin of victory was not greater. Two goals in as many minutes on the stroke of half-time by Origi and Sakho set the ball rolling. The visitors' cause was not helped by the dismissal of Funes Mori shortly after the break and the rampant Reds added to their woe with further goals from Sturridge and Coutinho.

Liverpool's FA Barclays Premier League results 2015/16

Date	Opponent		Score		Date	Opponent		Score
09.08.2015	Stoke City	(a)	1 - 0		02.01.2016	West Ham United	(a)	0 - 2
17.08.2015	Bournemouth	(h)	1 - 0		13.01.2016	Arsenal	(h)	3 - 3
24.08.2015	Arsenal	(a)	0 - 0		17.01.2016	Manchester United	(h)	0 - 1
29.08.2015	West Ham United	(h)	0 - 3		23.01.2016	Norwich City	(a)	5 - 4
12.09.2015	Manchester United	(a)	1 - 3		02.02.2016	Leicester City	(a)	0 - 2
20.09.2015	Norwich City	(h)	1 - 1		06.02.2016	Sunderland	(h)	2 - 2
26.09.2015	Aston Villa	(h)	3 - 2		14.02.2016	Aston Villa	(a)	6 - 0
04.10.2015	Everton	(a)	1 - 1		02.03.2016	Manchester City	(h)	3 - 0
17.10.2015	Tottenham Hotspur	(a)	0 - 0		06.03.2016	Crystal Palace	(a)	2 - 1
25.10.2015	Southampton	(h)	1 - 1		20.03.2016	Southampton	(a)	2 - 3
31.10.2015	Chelsea	(a)	3 - 1		02.04.2016	Tottenham Hotspur	(h)	1 - 1
08.11.2015	Crystal Palace	(h)	1 - 2		10.04.2016	Stoke City	(h)	4 - 1
21.11.2015	Manchester City	(a)	4 - 1		17.04.2016	Bournemouth	(a)	2 - 1
29.11.2015	Swansea City	(h)	1 - 0		20.04.2016	Everton	(h)	4 - 0
06.12.2015	Newcastle United	(a)	0 - 2		23.04.2016	Newcastle United	(h)	2 - 2
13.12.2015	West Bromwich Albion	(h)	2 - 2		01.05.2016	Swansea City	(a)	1 - 3
20.12.2015	Watford	(a)	0 - 3		08.05.2016	Watford	(h)	2 - 0
26.12.2015	Leicester City	(h)	1 - 0		11.05.2016	Chelsea	(h)	1 - 1
30.12.2015	Sunderland	(a)	1 - 0		15.05.2016	West Bromwich Albion	(a)	1 - 1

PLAYER PROFILES

Simon Mignolet

Position: Goalkeeper
Date of Birth: 6/3/1988
Birthplace: Sint-Truiden, Belgium
Signed from: Sunderland (June 2013)
Squad Number: 22

Loris Karius

Position: Goalkeeper
Date of Birth: 22/6/1993
Birthplace: Biberach, Germany
Signed from: Mainz 05 (May 2016)
Squad Number: 1

Nathaniel Clyne

Position: Defence
Date of Birth: 5/4/1991
Birthplace: Stockwell, England
Signed from: Southampton (July 2015)
Squad Number: 2

Joe Gomez

Position: Defence
Date of Birth: 23/5/1997
Birthplace: Catford, England
Signed from: Charlton Athletic (June 2015)
Squad Number: 12

THE ROAD TO WEMBLEY 2016

Within just four months of taking charge at Liverpool Jürgen Klopp led his team out in the Capital One Cup final. It was the club's 5th appearance at the new Wembley but it ultimately ended in disappointment with the Reds being denied a first trophy since 2012 by the narrowest of margins…

3rd round
Carlisle United (h) 1-1
*****won 3-2 on penalties**

The Capital One Cup run began has it would end, via the lottery of a penalty shoot-out. Against Carlisle United at Anfield Ings netted the opening goal only for the League Two minnows to hit back with an equaliser just 11 minutes later. That's how it remained and not even extra-time could then separate the two teams. It was a far from convincing performance from Brendan Rodgers' team but debutant Bogdán emerged the hero in the subsequent shoot-out – saving three spot-kicks as Liverpool scraped through.

4th round
Bournemouth (h) 1-0

Premier League Bournemouth provided the opposition in round four and, with Klopp now installed as manager, Liverpool advanced more comfortably. It was another tight game though, decided only by Clyne's first goal in a red shirt; the full-back, a close-season signing from Southampton, finding the back of the net in the 17th minute.

5th round
Southampton (a) 6-1

On paper, the trip to St Mary's at the quarter-final stage should have been Liverpool's sternest test yet on their Capital One Cup run. And so it seemed when they fell behind to a 1st minute goal. But the transformation thereafter was amazing, with two Sturridge goals and a first for Origi sending the Reds in at the interval 3-1 to the good. Origi went on to complete his hat-trick in the second half while Ibe also got in on the act as Southampton were completely overwhelmed.

Semi-final
Stoke City (a) 1-0
Stoke City (h) 0-1
*won 6-5 on penalties

With Wembley just one step away this two-legged semi-final was a tight, cagey, affair. In the first leg at the Britannia Stadium, Liverpool deservedly edged it thanks to Ibe's 37th minute strike. With home advantage in the second leg the Reds were favourites to progress but, again, it was the visitors who came out on top, Marko Arnautovic cancelling out Liverpool's first leg lead on the stroke of half-time. There was no further scoring in normal time or the extra half hour, and so, for the second time in the Capital One Cup that season, Anfield got to witness the drama of a penalty shoot-out. After five kicks each the teams were still level and it needed sudden death to determine the winners. When Mignolet saved from Muniesa, Allen then stepped forward to convert his penalty and book Liverpool's passage to Wembley.

Final
Manchester City (Wembley) 1-1
*lost 1-3 on penalties

After two penalty victories on the road to Wembley it was Liverpool's turn to suffer the heartache of a shoot-out loss as Manchester City claimed the first silverware of the season. In a closely fought encounter the Reds trailed to a 48th minute opening goal by Fernandinho but their persistence was eventually rewarded seven minutes from the end of normal time when Coutinho pounced to score on the rebound after Lallana had hit the post. Chances then came and went for both sides until the end of extra-time signalled yet another penalty shoot-out and this time it was to be a case of third time unlucky for the Reds, with Can the only player to convert. Lucas, Coutinho and Lallana all saw their efforts saved and dreams that the Klopp-era could get off to an early trophy-winning start were dashed.

MIGHTY RED'S PUZZLE PAGES

Liverpool FC's official mascot Mighty Red is on a problem solving mission.
See if you can help…

Goal!
Football is a team game so can you provide assistance and direct me along the right path to score?

Name the Year
Liverpool Football Club exists to win trophies and we've certainly won more than our fair share through the years. However, can you remember the year when these ones were lifted?

Answers on page 60 and 61.

Anagrams

We're lucky to have had so many legends play for this club.
Unscramble the following to reveal ten of the best...

LAGHDSIL

RGARDRE

SRNAEB

GENAKE

UZARES

BLRAGOABRE

NSLOAO

ACMMNAMNA

YHAPYI

RGACHERAR

For Club & Country

Can you match the Liverpool player with the flag of the country he represents?

Roberto Firmino

Sadio Mané

Divock Origi

Dejan Lovren

Nathaniel Clyne

Emre Can

Georginio Wijnaldum

Mamadou Sakho

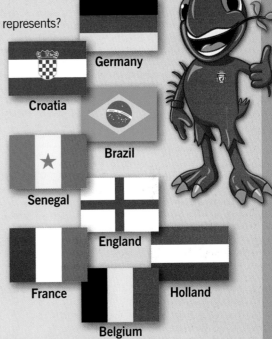

Germany

Croatia

Brazil

Senegal

England

France

Holland

Belgium

LFC's A-to-Z

Let's think of a Liverpool FC-themed **word**, **name** or **phrase** for each letter of the alphabet?

A	B	C
D	E	F
G	H	I
J	K	L
M	N	O
P	Q	R
S	T	U
V	W	X
Y	Z	

Answers on page 60 and 61.

MEET 'THE WORLD'S BIGGEST FOOTBALL FAMILY'

From Bootle to Boston, Kirkdale to Kuala Lumpur or Speke to the Seychelles – Liverpool Football Club's immense popularity stretches way beyond the confines of Merseyside. It reaches right around the globe.

As one of the world's best supported clubs, the Reds are able to boast a passionate following in almost every far flung corner of the planet.

With over 200 Official Supporters' Clubs, spread across six continents and 78 different countries, it adds up to a vast worldwide fan-base – one that Liverpool Football Club is extremely proud of.

But where in the world are you most likely to meet fellow members of the extended LFC family?

Here is a full list of countries in which there is at least one Official Liverpool Supporters Club...

North America

Canada (4)
Bermuda
USA (32)

Africa

Egypt
Kenya
Seychelles
Mauritius
Uganda
South Africa (4)

South America

Brazil
Argentina

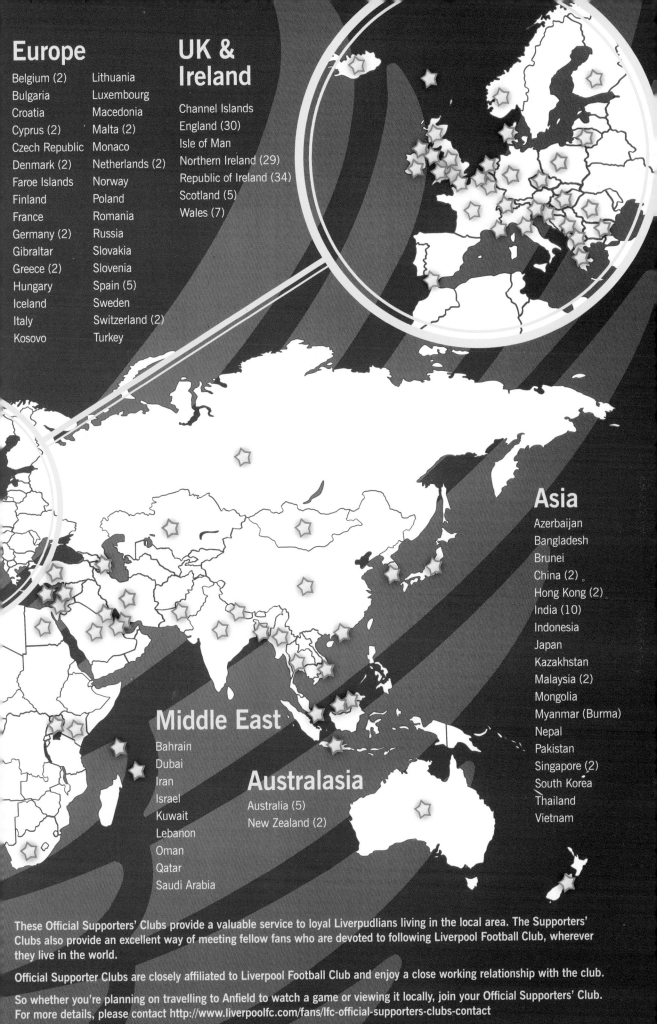

Europe

Belgium (2)	Lithuania
Bulgaria	Luxembourg
Croatia	Macedonia
Cyprus (2)	Malta (2)
Czech Republic	Monaco
Denmark (2)	Netherlands (2)
Faroe Islands	Norway
Finland	Poland
France	Romania
Germany (2)	Russia
Gibraltar	Slovakia
Greece (2)	Slovenia
Hungary	Spain (5)
Iceland	Sweden
Italy	Switzerland (2)
Kosovo	Turkey

UK & Ireland

Channel Islands
England (30)
Isle of Man
Northern Ireland (29)
Republic of Ireland (34)
Scotland (5)
Wales (7)

Asia

Azerbaijan
Bangladesh
Brunei
China (2)
Hong Kong (2)
India (10)
Indonesia
Japan
Kazakhstan
Malaysia (2)
Mongolia
Myanmar (Burma)
Nepal
Pakistan
Singapore (2)
South Korea
Thailand
Vietnam

Middle East

Bahrain
Dubai
Iran
Israel
Kuwait
Lebanon
Oman
Qatar
Saudi Arabia

Australasia

Australia (5)
New Zealand (2)

These Official Supporters' Clubs provide a valuable service to loyal Liverpudlians living in the local area. The Supporters' Clubs also provide an excellent way of meeting fellow fans who are devoted to following Liverpool Football Club, wherever they live in the world.

Official Supporter Clubs are closely affiliated to Liverpool Football Club and enjoy a close working relationship with the club.

So whether you're planning on travelling to Anfield to watch a game or viewing it locally, join your Official Supporters' Club. For more details, please contact http://www.liverpoolfc.com/fans/lfc-official-supporters-clubs-contact

50 CELEBRITY REDS...

From the world of TV, film, music and sport - how many of these famous names did you know supported Liverpool?

1. Daniel Craig (actor – James Bond)
2. Brad Pitt (actor – Fight Club, Moneyball)
3. Clive Owen (actor – Sin City, Children Of Men)
4. David Morrissey (actor – One Summer, Walking Dead)
5. John Bishop (comedian, TV presenter)
6. Gary Barlow (singer/songwriter – Take That)
7. Samuel L Jackson (actor – 51st State)
8. Mike Myers (actor – Wayne's World, Austin Powers)
9. Damian Lewis (actor – Homeland, Will)
10. Liam Neeson (actor – Schindlers List, Star Wars The Phantom Menace)
11. Gerry Marsden (singer/songwriter – Gerry & the Pacemakers)
12. Elvis Costello (singer/songwriter)
13. Mark Moraghan (actor – Brookside, Casualty)
14. Ricky Tomlinson (actor – Brookside, Royle Family)
15. Sue Johnston (actress – Brookside, Royle Family)
16. Adam Woodyatt (actor – Eastenders)
17. Craig Charles (actor – Red Dwarf, Coronation Street)
18. Les Dennis (TV presenter, actor, comedian)
19. Jason Isaacs (actor – Harry Potter)
20. Kirsty Gallacher (TV presenter – Sky Sports)
21. Kelly Cates (TV presenter – BT Sport)
22. Dr Dre (rapper)
23. Lana Del Rey (singer/songwriter)
24. DJ Spoony (DJ)
25. Chris De Burgh (singer/songwriter)
26. Kim Cattrall (actress – Sex & The City)
27. Mel C (former Spice Girl)
28. Angelina Jolie (actress – Lara Croft: Tomb Raider)
29. Jimmy McGovern (screenwriter, TV producer)
30. Jimmy Tarbuck (TV presenter, comedian)
31. Stan Boardman (comedian)
32. Pete Wylie (singer/songwriter – The Mighty Wah)
33. Ian McCulloch (singer/songwriter – Echo & The Bunnymen)
34. John Power (singer/songwriter – Cast)
35. Peter Hooton (singer/songwriter – The Farm)
36. Caroline Wozniacki (tennis player)
37. Darren Clarke (golfer)
38. James Walsh (singer/songwriter – Starsailor)
39. Danny Willett (golfer)
40. Simon Rimmer (chef)
41. LeBron James (basketballer)
42. Seamus (WWE Wrestler)
43. David Price (boxer)
44. Paul Smith (boxer)
45. Stephen Smith (boxer)
46. Liam Smith (boxer)
47. Callum Smith (boxer)
48. Stephen Bunting (darts player)
49. Russell Howard (comedian, TV presenter)
50. Andy Brown (singer/songwriter – Lawson)

SPOT THE DIFFERENCE

Have a close look at the two pictures below and see if you can spot the 10 differences...

Answers on page 60 and 61

PLAYER PROFILES

Connor Randall

Position: Defence
Date of birth: 21/10/1995
Birthplace: Liverpool, England
Signed from: Schoolboy (2003)
Squad Number: 56

Alberto Moreno

Position: Defence
Date of Birth: 5/7/1992
Birthplace: Seville, Spain
Signed from: Sevilla (August 2014)
Squad number: 18

Dejan Lovren

Position: Defence
Date of Birth: 5/7/1989
Birthplace: Zenica, Bosnia
& Herzegovina
Signed from: Southampton
(July 2014)
Squad Number: 6

Joël Matip

Position: Defence
Date of Birth: 8/8/1991
Birthplace: Bochum,
Germany
Signed from: Schalke 04
(July 2016)
Squad Number: 32

THE ROAD TO BASEL 2016

The undoubted on-pitch highlight of Liverpool's 2015/16 season was the exciting run to a 12th major European final. Defeat to Sevilla in Basel was a bitter pill to swallow but the memories of that Cup run will live long in our minds...

Group Stage
Bordeaux (a) 1-1 – Sion (h) 1-1 – Rubin Kazan (h) 1-1 – Rubin Kazan (a) 1-0 – Bordeaux (h) 2-1 – Sion (a) 0-0

The Europa League campaign began on a low key note with three successive 1-1 draws, the latter of which – at home to Rubin Kazan – being Jürgen Klopp's Anfield bow as Liverpool manager. A fortnight later, Jordon Ibe struck the only goal of the return with Kazan to register the Reds' first group win and victory over Bordeaux followed, meaning a goalless draw in the concluding fixture away to Sion was enough to secure qualification to the knockout stage.

Round of 32
Augsburg (a) 0-0
Augsburg (h) 1-0

Klopp took Liverpool to his native Germany for their first game of the knockout phase and the minnows from Augsburg proved to be stern opposition. A goalless draw in Bavaria left the tie finely balanced ahead of the second leg at Anfield the following week and only an early Milner penalty separated the sides.

Round of 16
Manchester United (h) 2-0
Manchester United (a) 1-1

When the draw paired Liverpool with arch rivals Manchester United the whole of Europe gasped. It was a tie that would have graced the Champions League and this first ever European meeting between the two giants of English football got everyone buzzing in anticipation. It didn't disappoint. The first leg took place at a raucous Anfield and Liverpool deservedly ran out 2-0 winners through goals from Sturridge and Firmino. Despite conceding a first half penalty in the return leg at Old Trafford it was Liverpool who controlled proceedings and when Coutinho levelled matters on the night shortly before the break, a famous aggregate victory was secured.

Quarter-final
Borussia Dortmund (a) 1-1
Borussia Dortmund (h) 4-3

If Klopp's return to Germany in the round of 32 was said to be emotional it was nothing compared to the reception that greeted him when he led the Reds into battle against his former club. With both sets of supporters creating an electric atmosphere at both legs, the tie was one to savour. In Dortmund, Origi fired Liverpool into a first-half lead, only for Hummels to equalise just three minutes after the interval. However, against a Borussia side that many were tipping to go all the way in the competition, the Reds had given a more than credible account of themselves. The German giants were a much different proposition in front of the Kop and showed their class by racing into a two-goal lead. Origi later pulled a goal back but when Reus added a third for the visitors Liverpool's Europa League run looked to be over. With a passionate home crowd roaring them on though, the Reds refused to accept defeat. What followed was one of the most remarkable comebacks in the club's history. Goals from Coutinho and Sakho squared the tie but as we entered injury time Dortmund were still going through on the away goals rule. Then, Lovren rose highest at the far post and headed home the most sensational of winners. Cue pandemonium on the pitch and in the stands. Liverpool had snatched a place in the last four on an unforgettable night that will forever rank as one of the best Anfield has ever seen.

Semi-final
Villarreal (a) 0-1
Villarreal (h) 3-0

After the drama of the previous round this semi-final tie was always going to be something of an anti-climax but nevertheless, despite suffering the body blow of losing to a last-gasp goal in the first-leg at El Madrigal, Liverpool eventually booked their place in the final with apparent ease. In front of another highly-charged Anfield crowd the Reds sunk the Yellow Submarine with a thoroughly professional performance at the second attempt. An own-goal by Soriano levelled the aggregate score after just seven minutes and the Villarreal players were visibly rocking but Liverpool bided their time before second half goals by Sturridge and Lallana clinched victory and a ticket to Basel.

Final
Sevilla (Basel) 1-3

Hopes were high that in Basel's St Jakob Park Liverpool could add another glorious chapter to its rich European history. Over 30,000 Liverpudlians travelled across Europe to support Klopp's Red Army in their quest to end the season on a high, vastly outnumbering those from Sevilla and creating another amazing atmosphere. When Sturridge fired the Reds into a half-time lead it should have been the cue for the parties to begin. Sevilla, however, were far from finished. The Spaniards were seeking to win the Europa League for a record-breaking fifth time. They'd lifted the trophy in the previous two seasons and we were about to see why. Within a minute of the second half starting they'd drawn level and by the 70th minute it was 3-1. Liverpool had no answer and Sevilla were fully deserving of their victory.

COMPETITION

Answer the following question correctly and you could win a Liverpool FC shirt signed by a first team player.

Q **How many European Cups/Champions Leagues have Liverpool FC won?**
a) 3   b) 5   c) 7

Entry is by email only. Only one entrant per contestant. Please enter LFC SHIRT followed by either A, B or C in the subject line of an email. In the body of the email, please include your full name, address, postcode, email address and phone number and send to:

frontdesk@grangecommunications.co.uk by Friday 24th March 2017.

Terms and Conditions

1) The closing date for this competition is Friday 24th March 2017 at midnight. Entries received after that time will not be counted.

2) Information on how to enter and on the prizes form part of these conditions.

3) Entry is open to those residing in the UK only. If entrants are under 18, consent from a parent or guardian must be obtained and the parent or guardian must agree to these terms and conditions.

4) This competition is not open to employees or their relatives of Liverpool FC. Any such entries will be invalid.

5) The start date for entries is 31st October 2016 at 4pm.

6) Entries must be strictly in accordance with these terms and conditions. Any entry not in strict accordance with these terms and conditions will be deemed to be invalid and no prizes will be awarded in respect of any such entry. By entering, all entrants will be deemed to accept these rules.

7) One (1) lucky winner will win a 2016/2017 season signed football shirt.

8) The prize is non-transferable and no cash alternative will be offered. Entry is by email only. Please enter LFC SHIRT followed by either A, B or C in the subject line of an email. In the body of the email, please include your full name, address, postcode, email address and phone number and send to: frontdesk@ grangecommunications.co.uk by Friday 24th March 2017.

9) The winner will be picked at random. The winner will be contacted within 72 hours of the closing date. Details of the winner can be requested after this time from the address below.

10) Entries must not be sent in through agents or third parties. No responsibility can be accepted for lost, delayed, incomplete, or for electronic entries or winning notifications that are not received or delivered. Any such entries will be deemed void.

11) The winners shall have 72 hours to claim their prize once initial contact has been made by the Promoter. Failure to respond may result in forfeiture of the prize.

12) On entering the competition you are allowing Liverpool Football Club and its trusted partners to contact you with information about products and services they believe might be of interest to you. If you do not wish to receive any marketing information from the Club, you can opt out by emailing LFC STOP to frontdesk@ grangecommunications.co.uk before midnight on Friday 24th March 2017.

13) The Promoter reserves the right to withdraw or amend the promotion as necessary due to circumstances outside its reasonable control. The Promoter's decision on all matters is final and no correspondence will be entered into.

14) The Promoter (or any third party nominated by the Promoter) may use the winner's name and image and their comments relating to the prize for future promotional, marketing and publicity purposes in any media worldwide without notice or without any fee being paid.

15) Liverpool Football Club's decision is final, no correspondence will be entered in to. Except in respect of death or personal injury resulting from any negligence of the Club, neither the Liverpool Football Club nor any of its officers, employees or agents shall be responsible for (whether in tort, contract or otherwise): (i) Any loss, damage or injury to you and/or any guest or to any property belonging to you or any guest in connection with this competition and / or the prize, resulting from any cause whatsoever; (ii) for any loss of profit, loss of use, loss of opportunity or any indirect, economic or consequential losses whatsoever.

16) This competition shall be governed by English law.

17) Promoter: Grange Communications, 22 Great King Street, Edinburgh, EH3 6QH

WORDSEARCH

There's no European football for Liverpool in 2016/17 but to help keep the Euro memories alive, can you find the names of 20 teams (listed below) that the Reds have faced in continental competition through the years?

B	R	U	G	E	S	W	M	I	L	A	N	R	R	K	G
I	H	I	B	E	R	N	I	A	N	F	F	J	Y	W	L
N	H	N	K	T	V	V	G	A	C	I	F	N	E	B	R
T	O	W	W	T	A	Z	X	V	G	O	M	L	A	M	Y
E	N	Y	M	H	Y	U	L	M	X	O	C	G	G	F	Q
R	V	M	K	C	M	W	X	A	Q	E	C	R	T	N	Q
N	E	F	K	E	R	E	J	E	L	T	U	A	R	F	X
A	D	D	I	L	W	A	L	T	R	B	Q	N	N	N	G
Z	N	V	V	R	R	Q	I	L	S	R	H	O	Y	O	Z
I	C	A	A	E	B	C	J	G	I	A	E	L	H	Z	M
O	K	L	J	D	D	R	U	K	M	E	Y	E	N	B	W
N	P	E	K	N	T	A	O	B	N	W	S	C	M	Y	D
A	T	N	Y	A	F	B	U	N	A	Y	M	R	M	B	T
L	R	C	E	T	T	R	D	M	D	R	C	A	A	Z	Q
E	H	I	R	Y	G	T	O	V	J	B	R	B	M	M	C
X	X	A	Q	C	N	R	N	H	P	D	Y	M	M	N	X

Ajax
Anderlecht
Augsburg
Auxerre
Barcelona
Benfica
Brondby
Bruges
Celtic
Hamburg

Hibernian
Honved
Internazionale
Malmo
Marseille
Milan
Monaco
Reykjavik
Roma
Valencia

Answers on page 60 and 61.

LFC LADIES IN SOUTH AFRICA

In February 2016 Liverpool Ladies embarked on a momentous, week-long, two-game, pre-season tour to South Africa and goalkeeper Siobhan Chamberlain kept this diary of what turned out to be an unforgettable trip…

Saturday

After about 24 hours of travelling it was lovely to be greeted by a group of Liverpool supporters when we arrived at the hotel in Johannesburg, singing and cheering as we got off the bus. We didn't have much time to relax before we were put to work and manager Scott Rogers kindly reminded us that we 'weren't on holiday' as we all got a little excited about the sunshine! Training that afternoon was only very light but it was good to get the travelling out of our system and have a look at the pitch we'd be playing on the following day. The Soweto Nike Training Centre is a fantastic venue for the area and great to give youngsters there the opportunity to play football every day.

Sunday

The morning was meant to be a chilled-out team challenge, but given the competitive nature of us all it turned into sprinting through corridors and an incredibly competitive morning. Of course my team won but we're still waiting for our prize! Although we'd only arrived the day before, today was game-day and we had a 60-minute training match against Yarona Ladies. It was an important test for us ahead of Wednesday's big match.

Playing in the 30-degree heat when you're used to freezing English conditions is hard enough, but throw in the altitude and a challenging surface and it definitely made things difficult! After going down 1-0 we showed great character to win the game 2-1 with late goals from Caroline Weir and Katie Zelem. Not the best of performances but it was important to get the win and we managed to grind out the result!

Monday

Not your average day as a footballer. It started off fairly normal with a morning training session, but the afternoon was a slightly different affair. Some of us took part in a photo-shoot for the South African Sunday Times. It was great fun having our hair and make-up done professionally, although some of the outfits were 'interesting' to say the least. Don't expect anything you see to be on a high street near you any time soon!

Tuesday

Probably one of the most heart-rending experiences a lot of us have had in our football careers. After another morning training session we headed down to Alexandra, one of the worst-off townships in South Africa. We met 40 young girls who love football and got involved in a coaching session with them. It was amazing to see how football can bring people together from all walks of life and can give people from disadvantaged areas the chance to aspire to reach their dreams. To tour South Africa was a fantastic opportunity, but to be able to give back to the local communities was even more important and I think we probably enjoyed it as much as the kids did.

Wednesday

It's not often you have a jam-packed schedule on a matchday, but when you're in a country with so much to offer it's impossible to fit it all in. Wednesday morning was pretty busy to say the least but a day I'm sure none of us will ever forget! It was an absolute honour to be invited to visit the Nelson Mandela Foundation and be shown around his office and museum. We were then able to go and visit the Lion Park. I don't think you can go to South Africa without going on Safari. Travelling round the park we saw lions, zebras, and cheetahs and then even got to cuddle a baby lion cub and feed a giraffe. Not your average matchday prep!

The match that night at the Soweto Nike Football Centre didn't get off to the best of starts. We got stuck in Johannesburg rush-hour traffic so they had to delay kick-off, the pitch was waterlogged and then, against the run of play, we were 2-0 down at half-time. However, a sign of any good team is how they react to adversity and our second-half performance was pretty impressive, coming back to win 6-2!

I must add a special thank you to all of the youngsters from Waterstone College who helped to clear the pitch as well as the Liverpool supporters that came to watch and sang their hearts out throughout – it definitely made a difference.

Thursday

You don't often get recovery days in 30-degree sunshine and an outdoor pool so it's safe to say we made the most of our final morning in South Africa. I don't think anyone had been so keen to get in the pool and stretch! However, a couple of hours later and we had the loudest thunderstorm I'd ever heard – probably a saving grace for the pasty ones of the group who had turned a little red! The trip finished with a team lunch at a local South African restaurant and some traditional face-painting. Quite an end to a great tour.

PLAYER PROFILES

Mamadou Sakho

Position: Defence
Date of Birth: 13/2/1990
Birthplace: Paris, France
Signed from: Paris St Germain
(September 2013)
Squad Number: 3

Ragnar Klavan

Position: Defence
Date of Birth: 30/10/1985
Birthplace: Viljandi, Estonia
Signed from: Augsburg (July 2016)
Squad Number: 17

Lucas Leiva

Position: Midfield
Date of Birth: 9/1/1987
Birthplace: Dourados, Brazil
Signed from: Gremio
(May 2007)
Squad Number: 21

James Milner

Position: Midfield
Date of Birth: 4/1/1986
Birthplace: Horsforth, England
Signed from: Manchester City
(July 2015)
Squad Number: 7

DOT-TO-DOT

Join the dots in numerical order and discover what the pattern reveals.

HAPPY 125TH BIRTHDAY LFC

In June 2017 Liverpool Football Club will celebrate its 125th birthday. To commemorate this landmark anniversary we recall 125 milestone moments in LFC history…

1. Liverpool Football Club is officially born, with John Houlding its founding chairman (June 1892)

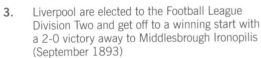

2. The new club play their first competitive match and mark the occasion with an 8-0 rout of Higher Walton in the Lancashire League (September 1892)

3. Liverpool are elected to the Football League Division Two and get off to a winning start with a 2-0 victory away to Middlesbrough Ironopilis (September 1893)

4. Promotion to the top-flight is secured at the first attempt courtesy of a 2-0 Test Match success against Newton Heath (April 1894)

5. The Reds record what remains their highest-ever victory in League football as Rotherham Town are pummelled 10-1 at Anfield (February 1896)

6. The club's first superstar player Alex Raisbeck joins the club for £350 from Stoke City (May 1898)

7. The highly-regarded Tom Watson is recruited from Sunderland as secretary-manager (August 1896)

8. Liverpool are crowned champions of England for the first time (April 1901)

9. The title returns to Anfield as the Reds finish the season four points ahead of nearest challengers Preston (April 1906)

10. Renowned architect Archibald Leitch is hired to oversee an extensive redevelopment of Anfield, with new stands being erected on three sides of the ground – including the Kop (May 1906)

11. Legendary goalkeeper Elisha Scott makes his senior Liverpool debut and keeps a clean sheet in a goalless draw away at Newcastle (January 1913)

12. Liverpool reach the FA Cup Final for the first time but lose 1-0 to Burnley at Crystal Palace (April 1914)

13. Liverpool embark on their first foreign tour with a five-game end-of-season trip to Scandinavia (May 1914)

14. Liverpool clinch the First Division Championship for a third time following a 2-1 home defeat of Burnley (April 1922)

15. Liverpool complete back-to-back title triumphs (May 1923)

16. Liverpool sign up their first ever foreign player when South African goalkeeper Arthur Riley arrives from Boksburg FC (August 1925)

17. A roof is put on the Spion Kop, making it one of the most atmospheric terraces in world football (August 1928)

18. Gordon Hodgson registers his club record 17th and final hat-trick in a Liverpool shirt (February 1935)

19. Liverpool beat Everton 6-0 at Anfield in what is still their best-ever derby win (September 1935)

20. Jack Balmer scores what is genuinely regarded as the quickest-ever Liverpool goal when he nets after just ten seconds of the 3-1 derby win at Goodison (February 1938)

21. Billy Liddell scores his first competitive Liverpool goal as the Reds come out on top in a sensational eleven goal Anfield thriller against Chelsea (September 1946)

22. Albert Stubbins joins the Reds in a record-breaking transfer deal from Newcastle United (September 1946)

23. Jack Balmer creates history by scoring three consecutive hat-tricks (November 1946)

24. Liverpool are confirmed as the inaugural post-war champions after Stoke fail to defeat Sheffield United in their final league game of an extended season (June 1947)

25. Liverpool's first visit to Wembley ends in disappointment as Arsenal run out 2-0 winners to take the FA Cup (April 1950)

26. A patch of land is purchased in West Derby and converted into what we now know as the club's Melwood training base (1950)

27. Anfield's all-time record attendance of 61,905 is set when Wolves visit for a FA Cup fourth round tie (February 1952)

28. Liverpool suffer the indignity of relegation from the top-flight for the third time in their history after finishing bottom of the pile with just 28 points (April 1954)

29. Liverpool endure their heaviest-ever defeat as Birmingham City romp to a 9-1 success at St Andrews (December 1954)

30. Second Division Liverpool cause the shock of the FA Cup 4th round with a resounding 4-0 victory over their top-flight Mersey neighbours Everton at Goodison Park (January 1955)

31. The floodlights are switched on at Anfield for the first time as the Reds host Everton in a friendly to commemorate the 75th anniversary of the Liverpool County FA (October 1957)

32. Liverpool suffer their most humiliating-ever defeat in the third round of the FA Cup to non-league Worcester City (January 1959)

33. Bill Shankly is appointed as manager at Anfield (December 1959)

34. All-time record appearance holder Ian Callaghan makes his Liverpool debut and stars in a 4-1 Anfield win over Bristol Rovers (April 1959)

35. Liverpool smash their transfer record by forking out £37,500 to capture Motherwell forward Ian St John (May 1961)

36. A Kevin Lewis double in a 2-0 home win over Southampton confirms promotion, ending Liverpool's eight-year exile in Division Two (April 1962)

37. You'll Never Walk Alone tops the British music charts and is ad opted as the Kop's unofficial anthem (October 1963)

38. A 5-0 home win over Arsenal clinches Liverpool's 6th First Division Championship (April 1964)

39. Liverpool play in a European competition for the first time and mark the occasion with a 5-0 rout of Reykjavik in Iceland (August 1964)

40. Liverpool sport their now famous all-red strip for the first time in a European Cup tie at home to Anderlecht (November 1964)

41. The FA Cup is won for the first time as Leeds United are beaten on a historic afternoon at Wembley (May 1965)

42. Liverpool reclaim their mantle as English champions following a 2-1 home win over Chelsea (April 1966)

43. In their first-ever European final the Reds miss out on the Cup Winners' Cup following a 2-1 loss to Borussia Dortmund at Hampden Park (May 1966)

44. Champions Liverpool win the Charity Shield outright for the first time courtesy of a 1-0 win over FA Cup winners Everton at Goodison (August 1966)

45. Kevin Keegan scores in front of the Kop on his debut as Liverpool record an opening day 3-1 success against Nottingham Forest (August 1971)

46. Liverpool are crowned champions for a seventh time (April 1973)

47. Europe is conquered for the first time as Borussia Mönchengladbach are beaten over two legs in the final of the UEFA Cup (May 1973)

48. Liverpool win the FA Cup for a second time following a comprehensive 3-0 thrashing of Newcastle at Wembley (May 1974)

49. Bill Shankly sensationally announces his resignation as Liverpool manager (July 1974)

50. Bob Paisley reluctantly accepts to take over the Anfield managerial reigns (July 1974)

51. Liverpool chalk up their best ever victory with an 11-0 rout of Stromsgodset Drammen in a first round European Cup Winners' Cup tie at Anfield (September 1974)

52. A thrilling 3-1 victory over Wolves at Molineux clinches a 9th Championship success (May 1976)

53. FC Bruges are beaten over two legs as the UEFA Cup is won for a second time (May 1976)

54. David Fairclough scores one of Anfield's most celebrated goals as French champions St Etienne are famously defeated in the European Cup quarter-final (March 1977)

55. A goalless draw at home to West Ham is enough to secure a 10th League crown for the Reds (May 1977)

56. Liverpool beat Borussia Mönchengladbach 3-1 in Rome to win the European Cup for the first time (May 1977)

57. Kenny Dalglish joins Liverpool for a British record £440,000 from Celtic (August 1977)

58. A Terry McDermott hat-trick inspires a 6-0 rout of SV Hamburg as Liverpool clinch the European Super Cup for the first time (December 1977)

59. Liverpool reach the League Cup final for the first time but, following a goalless draw at Wembley, they are defeated 1-0 by Nottingham Forest in an Old Trafford replay (March 1978)

60. Liverpool become the first English club to retain the European Cup courtesy of a 1-0 victory over FC Bruges at Wembley (May 1978)

61. A 3-0 Anfield victory over Aston Villa confirms Liverpool's 11th League title (May 1979)

62. Avi Cohen scores for both teams as Liverpool beat Aston Villa 4-1 at Anfield to clinch a 12th First Division title (May 1980)

63. Liverpool bury their League Cup hoodoo with a 2-1 victory over West Ham in a replayed final at Villa Park (April 1981)

64. Alan Kennedy is an unlikely goalscoring hero as Liverpool defeat Real Madrid 1-0 in Paris to win a third European Cup (May 1981)

65. Liverpool set a new club transfer record to sign Brighton and Hove Albion defender Mark Lawrenson for £900,000 (August 1981)

66. Goals from Ronnie Whelan (2) and Ian Rush see Liverpool come from behind to retain the League Cup with a 3-1 victory over Tottenham at Wembley (March 1982)

67. Liverpool celebrate a 13th title triumph in front of the Kop as Spurs are beaten 3-1 on the final Saturday of the league season (May 1982)

68. Ian Rush scores four times at Goodison as Liverpool hammer Everton 5-0 to register their biggest away win in the Merseyside derby (November 1982)

69. Bob Paisley becomes the first manager to go up the steps at Wembley and collect a trophy as Liverpool win the League (Milk) Cup for a third successive season courtesy of a 2-1 win after extra-time in the final against Manchester United (March 1983)

70. Bob Paisley bows out as Liverpool manager after leading the Reds to a 14th First Division title (May 1983)

71. Backroom stalwart Joe Fagan succeeds Paisley as manager (June 1983)

72. Liverpool and Everton compete in the first all-Merseyside Wembley final but it takes a solitary Graeme Souness strike in the Maine Road replay to decide the destiny of the Milk Cup (March 1984)

73. A goalless draw against Notts County at Meadow Lane is enough to confirm a 15th League Championship triumph (May 1984)

74. Alan Kennedy's successful penalty conversion clinches a dramatic shoot-out victory over AS Roma in Rome and a fourth European Cup for the club (May 1984)

75. A grief-stricken Joe Fagan steps down as Liverpool boss after the Heysel Stadium disaster, in which 39 fans are killed prior to the European Cup Final defeat by Juventus (May 1985)

76. Player/boss Kenny Dalglish scores the only goal of the game to clinch a 16th title at Stamford Bridge (May 1986)

77. Everton are beaten in the FA Cup final at Wembley as the double is secured (May 1986)

78. Liverpool break their transfer record to capture the signature of Newcastle United's Peter Beardsley, paying the Geordies £1.9 million (July 1987)

79. After going 29 games unbeaten from the start of the season a 1-0 home win over Tottenham confirms a 17th League Championship triumph (April 1988)

80. John Aldridge becomes the first player to miss a penalty in the FA Cup final as the Reds are surprisingly defeated 1-0 at Wembley by Wimbledon, quashing dreams of a second double (May 1988)

81. After just one season with Juventus Ian Rush re-signs for the Reds (August 1988)

82. 96 Liverpool fans are tragically killed at Hillsborough as a result of crushing on the Leppings Lane terrace at the start of the FA Cup semi-final against Nottingham Forest (April 1989)

83. Ian Rush comes off the bench to net twice as Liverpool defeat Everton 3-2 in an emotionally-charged FA Cup final at Wembley (May 1989)

84. A last-gasp Michael Thomas strike denies Liverpool a second double and secures the title for Arsenal on a dramatic night at Anfield (May 1989)

85. A 2-1 home win against Queens Park Rangers sees Liverpool clinch an 18th League Championship (April 1990)

86. Kenny Dalglish sensationally announces that he's stepping down as Liverpool manager (February 1991)

87. Former skipper Graeme Souness is unveiled as Liverpool manager (April 1991)

88. Michael Thomas and Ian Rush are on the scoresheet as Liverpool beat Sunderland 2-0 at Wembley to win the FA Cup for a 5th time (May 1992)

89. Ian Rush becomes the club's all-time record goalscorer (October 1992)

90. Teenage striking sensation Robbie Fowler nets five times on his Anfield debut in a League Cup tie against Fulham (October 1993)

91. A shock 1-0 home defeat to Bristol City in an FA Cup third round replay is the prelude to Graeme Souness stepping down from his post as Reds boss (January 1994)

92. Boot-room boy Roy Evans replaces Souness as Liverpool manager (January 1994)

93. Fans stand on the Kop for a final time before it's demolished to make way for an all-seater grandstand (April 1994)

94. Robbie Fowler scores the then fastest hat-trick in Premier League history as Liverpool defeat Arsenal 3-0 at Anfield (August 1994)

95. A Steve McManaman double inspires Liverpool to victory over Bolton Wanderers in the Coca-Cola Cup final at Wembley (April 1995)

96. Inspired by a young Michael Owen and Jamie Carragher, Liverpool win the FA Youth Cup for the first time with a two-legged triumph over West Ham (May 1996)

97. Anfield plays host to four games in the Euro 96 tournament (June 1996)

98. Michael Owen makes his senior debut against Wimbledon at Selhurst Park and nets to become the club's youngest ever goalscorer (May 1997)

99. In a ground-breaking move by the club, Frenchman Gerard Houllier is appointed joint-manager of the Reds alongside Roy Evans (July 1998)

100. The doors are opened on the club's purpose-built youth Academy in Kirkby (1998)

101. Future captain Steven Gerrard makes his team debut as a late substitute at home to Blackburn Rovers (November 1998)

102. Liverpool celebrate their first appearance at Cardiff's Millennium Stadium by defeating Birmingham City on penalties to win the Worthington Cup (February 2001)

103. Michael Owen snatches the FA Cup from Arsenal's grasp with a late brace of goals as Liverpool come from behind to win 2-1 at the Millennium Stadium in Cardiff (May 2001)

104. On a thrilling night in Dortmund Liverpool complete an unprecedented cup treble with a thrilling 5-4 victory over Alaves in the greatest UEFA Cup final of all-time (May 2001)

105. Liverpool manager Gerard Houllier suffers a heart-attack at Anfield during the half-time interval of a Premier League game with Leeds (October 2001)

106. Michael Owen becomes the first Liverpool player to win the coveted Ballon D'Or (European Footballer of the Year) (December 2001)

107. Goals from Steven Gerrard and Michael Owen seal a 2-0 Worthington Cup final success over Manchester United in Cardiff (March 2003)

108. Rafael Benitez is unveiled as the new Reds boss (June 2004)

109. Liverpool stage the most heroic ever comeback to win the Champions League on penalties after trailing AC Milan 3-0 at the interval in Istanbul (May 2005)

110. In one of the most exciting FA Cup finals of all-time Liverpool fight-back to 3-3 against West Ham before taking the cup on penalties (May 2006)

111. George Gillett and Tom Hicks take control of the club (March 2007)

112. Liverpool compete in their seventh European Cup final but a brace of goals from Pippo Inzaghi condemns them to a 2-1 defeat in Athens (May 2007)

113. New club record signing Fernando Torres marks his Anfield debut with a goal of sublime class in a 1-1 draw with Chelsea (August 2007)

114. The managerial reign of Rafa Benitez comes to an end by mutual consent (June 2010)

115. Fulham boss Roy Hodgson is unveiled as Liverpool's new manager (July 2010)

116. Following a dramatic courtroom battle New England Sports Ventures (NESV) end months of uncertainty by completing their purchase of the club (October 2010)

117. Roy Hodgson's brief spell at the Anfield helm is brought to an end (January 2011)

118. Kenny Dalglish returns for his second stint as Liverpool manager (January 2011)

119. A dramatic transfer deadline day sees two club records smashed as Fernando Torres leaves for Chelsea and Andy Carroll signs from Newcastle (January 2011)

120. Luis Suarez comes off the bench to score on his Liverpool debut at home to Stoke City (February 2011)

121. On their first visit to the new Wembley Liverpool defeat Cardiff City on penalties to win the Carling Cup, the club's eighth triumph in the competition (February 2012)

122. Northern Irishman Brendan Rodgers is installed as the club's 14th post-war manager (July 2012)

123. Liverpool's talismanic and longest-serving captain Steven Gerrard plays his last game for the club (May 2015)

124. Jürgen Klopp is appointed Liverpool manager (October 2015)

125. Liverpool's redeveloped Main Stand is officially opened, increasing the overall capacity of Anfield to 54,000 (September 2016)

A SEASON IN NUMBERS

Club statistician Ged Rea picks out some key facts and figures from an eventful 2015/16 campaign for the Reds...

3 Three Liverpool players were sent off during the season - Philippe Coutinho, James Milner and Brad Smith.

4 Liverpool recorded league doubles over Aston Villa, Bournemouth, Manchester City and Stoke City.

5 The Reds found the net with all five penalties in normal time - James Milner scoring three. Christian Benteke and Daniel Sturridge bagging one each.

6 The number of times Liverpool came from behind to win a game, including twice in Europe - against Bordeaux and Borussia Dortmund.

7 The Reds failed to beat seven teams in the Barclays Premier League.

8 Philippe Coutinho scored eight times away from Anfield - more than any other Reds player.

12 Emre Can received more yellow cards in all games than any other Liverpool player.

12 The longest run of games that Liverpool went unbeaten - from the middle of September to early November.

12 A dozen players scored their first goal for Liverpool.

18 The second highest number of goals ever scored by substitutes during a season - six of which came from Christian Benteke.

19 Players made their debut for Liverpool during the 63-game campaign.

21 Clean sheets were kept by the club - 20 with Simon Mignolet between the sticks and the other with Adam Bogdan in goal.

22 Liverpool set a new club record with 22 different players finding the net. Daniel Sturridge, with 13, scored the most.

24 James Milner captained Liverpool more times than any other player - once more than Jordan Henderson.

25 Liverpool played 25 cup games during 2015-16, winning 11 of them with nine draws and five defeats.

31 Jordon Ibe was named as a substitute more times than any other Reds player, coming off the bench 21 times.

42 In total, 42 different players were named in matchday squads, with 39 of those taking to the field. Only Daniel Cleary, Conor Masterson and Ryan Fulton did not make an appearance.

52 The number of games Liverpool played under Jürgen Klopp. The Reds won 23 of them.

55 Simon Mignolet played more games than any other player for the club this season. The outfielder who appeared most was Nathaniel Clyne on 52 occasions.

63 The 63 times that the Reds took to the field was their highest since they also played 63 in 2000-01.

66 The number of seconds it took James Milner to score Liverpool's quickest goal of the season (against Aston Villa in September).

98 The total number of goals Liverpool scored in all competitions. The first came from Philippe Coutinho at Stoke; the last was scored by Daniel Sturridge in Basel.

44,228 The biggest Anfield attendance witnessed during the season was for a 3-2 win over Aston Villa in September.

PLAYER PROFILES

Emre Can

Position: Midfield
Date of Birth: 12/1/1994
Birthplace: Frankfurt, Germany
Signed from: Bayer Leverkusen (July 2014)
Squad Number:23

Georginio Wijnaldum

Position: Midfield
Date of Birth: 11/11/1990
Birthplace: Rotterdam, Holland
Signed from: Newcastle United (July 2016)
Squad Number: 5

Adam Lallana

Position: Midfield
Date of Birth: 10/5/1988
Birthplace: St Albans, England
Signed from: Southampton (July 2014)
Squad Number: 20

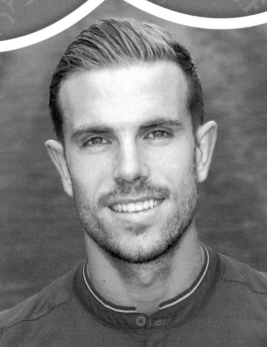

Jordan Henderson

Position: Midfield
Date of Birth: 17/6/1990
Birthplace: Sunderland, England
Signed from: Sunderland (June 2011)
Squad Number: 14

KNOW YOUR TEAM

Put your knowledge of the Reds to the test. There's a point on offer for each correct answer...

Know Your Team

1. From which club did the Reds sign Marko Grujić?

2. How many goals did Sadio Mané score against Liverpool last season?

3. Which Liverpool player began his professional career with Tonbense FC?

4. Who did Jürgen Klopp sign from his former club Mainz 05 in June 2016?

5. Against which club did Danny Ings score his first Liverpool goal?

6. Who was the only Liverpool player to score in the 2016 Capital One Cup final penalty shoot-out against Manchester City?

7. Which Liverpool player was named in the Euro 2016 team of the tournament?

8. Name the Liverpool player who has plied his trade in Brazil, Italy, Spain and England?

9. On what ground did Divock Origi score a hat-trick in December 2015?

10. Who scored Liverpool's last gasp winner in the dramatic 5-4 victory at Carrow Road in January 2016?

11. Which current Liverpool player scored against Brazil in the 2014 World Cup?

12. During his time with Sunderland, which lower league club did Jordan Henderson spend a loan period with?

13. In what year did Lucas Leiva sign for the Reds?

14. Who was the only Liverpool player to score a goal at Euro 2016?

15. Which Liverpool player joined Huddersfield Town on loan in July 2016?

True or False?

Daniel Sturridge started his career with Manchester City

| TRUE | ☐ | FALSE | ☐ |

Jon Flanagan was a boyhood Evertonian

| TRUE | ☐ | FALSE | ☐ |

Jürgen Klopp once played for Bayern Munich

| TRUE | ☐ | FALSE | ☐ |

Anfield has a bigger capacity than the Parc de Prince in Paris

| TRUE | ☐ | FALSE | ☐ |

Fill in the Blanks

Prior to signing for Liverpool James Milner played for Leeds, Newcastle United, _____, and Manchester City.

Liverpool fielded five debutants in the FA Cup third round tie at Exeter last season – Sheyi Ojo, Kevin Stewart, Tiago Ilori, Ryan Kent and _____.

During Liverpool's run to the 2016 Europa League final they defeated Augsburg, Manchester United, _____ and Villarreal in the knockout rounds.

Odd One Out

Which club have Liverpool not met in a European final – AS Roma, FC Bruges, Atletico Madrid, Borussia Monchengladbach, Sevilla?

Who was Liverpool's only representative at the 2016 Copa America – Roberto Firmino, Philippe Coutinho, Daniel Sturridge, Kolo Toure, Lucas Leiva?

In which country did Liverpool not play Europa League fixture in 2015/16 – Spain, Germany, France, Italy, Russia?

Penalty Prize

You've got five chances from the spot to gain some extra points. Simply guess if the following penalties were scored or missed....

Luis Suarez v Sunderland (h) Premier League, 13 August 2011

Mario Balotelli v Besiktas (h) Europa League round of 32, 19 February 2015

Steven Gerrard v Queens Park Rangers (h) Premier League, 2 May 2015

Daniel Sturridge v Manchester United (h) Europa League round of 16, 10 March 2016

Christian Benteke v Crystal Palace (a) Premier League, 16 March 2016

How many points did you score?

30 out of 30 – player of the season

25-29 – first team regular

15-20 – substitute

10-15 – in the reserves

10 and under – on the transfer list

Answers on page 60 and 61.

ON THE
INTERNATIONAL STAGE

For a number of Liverpool players the summer of 2016 was an extremely busy one. For them, there wasn't much time to switch off and relax on a far-away beach. As soon as the domestic season finished they were whisked away to join up with their countries in preparation for either the European Championship or Copa America. Here's how the Reds' international contingent fared...

Divock Origi, Christian Benteke, Simon Mignolet – BELGIUM – Euro 2016

One of the pre-tournament favourites, Belgium went as far as the quarter-finals before losing to Wales. Origi and Benteke each made two substitute appearances, while Mignolet was an unused substitute in all five matches.

Philippe Coutinho – BRAZIL – Copa America Centenario

Despite scoring the first international hat-trick of his career during Brazil's 7-1 destruction of Haiti in Orlando, Coutinho's bid for glory in the Copa America floundered at the first group phase. The 'Little Magician' played in all three games for Brazil but a goalless draw with Ecuador and 1-0 defeat to Peru meant the five-time world champions surprisingly bowed out early.

Daniel Sturridge, Adam Lallana, Nathaniel Clyne, Jordan Henderson, James Milner – ENGLAND – Euro 2016

Liverpool had more representatives in the England squad than any club other than Tottenham but it proved to be a disappointing tournament for those called up by Roy Hodgson. Sturridge's last-gasp winner in the group game with Wales was the undoubted highlight of a Three Lions' campaign that ended with a humiliating defeat to Iceland in the round of 16. All five of the Reds' contingent featured at least once; Sturridge and Lallana in three of the four games, while Henderson, Clyne and Milner each made just a solitary appearance.

Emre Can – GERMANY – Euro 2016

An unused substitute until the semi-final, Can was handed a start against the hosts in Marseille but, with Germany chasing the game after falling behind to a penalty on the stroke of half-time, he was replaced in the 67th minute by the more attack-minded Gotze. France went on to win 2-0 and the reigning world champions were out.

Martin Skrtel – SLOVAKIA – Euro 2016

Skrtel experienced mixed fortunes at Euro 2016. He captained Slovakia in all four of their games and his man-of-the-match performance in the goalless draw with England was a contributory factor in securing qualification from the group phase. However, any aspirations of further progression were promptly dealt a fatal blow when they lost 3-0 to Germany in the first knockout round.

Joe Allen, Danny Ward – WALES – Euro 2016

The surprise package of the tournament, Wales defied the odds to reach the last four in France – their best showing on the international stage since the 1958 World Cup. Allen started every game and earned rave reviews for his performances in midfield, while rookie keeper Ward was drafted in at the last minute to start Wales' first match before returning to the bench for the remainder of the tournament.

PLAYER PROFILES

Philippe Coutinho

Position: Midfield
Date of Birth: 12/6/1992
Birthplace: Rio de Janeiro, Brazil
Signed from: Inter Milan (January 2013)
Squad Number: 10

Marko Grujić

Position: Midfield
Date of Birth: 13/4/1996
Birthplace: Belgrade, Serbia
Signed from: Red Star Belgrade (January 2016)
Squad Number: 16

Roberto Firmino

Position: Forward
Date of Birth: 2/10/1991
Birthplace: Maceió, Brazil
Signed from: Hoffenheim
(July 2015)
Squad Number: 11

Sadio Mané

Position: Forward
Date of Birth: 10/4/1992
Birthplace: Sédhiou, Senegal
Signed from: Southampton
(July 2016)
Squad Number: 19

SPOT THE BALL

Can you place the missing ball in its correct position?

Answer on page 61.

THE OTHER LFC

Did you know that there are two Liverpool Football Clubs in this world? Almost seven thousand miles separate us and, while we're not exactly identical twins, here are some interesting facts about the team that share our famous name...

- The 'other Liverpool' are based in Uruguay, South America

- The club was formed on 15 February 1915 by a group of students in the country's capital Montevideo

- The reason they chose the name Liverpool was because of English football's popularity in Uruguay at the time and the then strong shipping links between the two cities

- Liverpool joined the Uruguayan Primera Division in 1919

- Throughout their 101 year history, they've not enjoyed much success, regularly flirting between the top two divisions and never winning their domestic championship

- They are one of 13 top-flight clubs in Montevideo and, like most, are constantly cast in the shadow of their more illustrious city rivals Penarol and Nacional

- Their first honour of note was the Uruguayan Segunda Division, won in 1966 and they've since claimed that title a further three times 1987, 2002 and 2015

- Liverpool's highest finishing place in the Uruguayan Primera Division is second, a feat they achieved in the 2003 Torneo Clausura

- They have competed in the Copa Libertadores (South America's version of the Champions League) on just one occasion, bowing at the first hurdle in 2011, and Copa Sudamericana (South America's version of the Europa League) twice

- The Uruguayan Liverpool have never met a team from England but once toured Europe in 1971

- Home games are played at the 10,000 capacity Estadio Belvedere where flags bearing the initials of our famous anthem 'YNWA' are often on display

- In 2012 Paul McCartney became an honorary member of the club

- The Uruguayan Liverpool play in blue and black striped shirts, similar to Inter Milan. These have been their colours since formation, hence the nickname 'Negriazules' (blue and blacks)

- In 2005/06, following our Champions League triumph in Istanbul, they temporarily adopted all-red as their away colours

- A further connection between the two Liverpools centres around our former number seven Luis Suarez, who was brought to the attention of scouts from Groningen (his first European club) after they had initially travelled to the Belvedere to watch Liverpool striker Elias Figueroa

- And finally, while it's unlikely that the two Liverpool teams will ever meet in a competitive fixture, it's not completely impossible. For such a scenario to unfold both clubs would first need to be crowned champions of their respective continents before potentially facing each other in the FIFA Club World Cup. You never know!

REDS ON TOUR 2016

The summer of 2016 was another busy one for the Liverpool first team squad as they prepared for the current campaign, with games in England, USA and Germany.

A short trip across the River Mersey kicked off the pre-season programme and a 1-0 victory over Tranmere Rovers was followed by three more wins on the road against lower league opposition in the shape of Fleetwood Town (5-0), Wigan Athletic (2-0) and Huddersfield Town (2-0).

Next up was the club's 8th tour of America and it was to the West Coast that the team headed. Stanford University in California was their training base but at the Rose Bowl Stadium in Pasadena, venue of the 1994 World Cup final, the Reds suffered a 1-0 loss to Chelsea in their opening game of the International Champions Cup.

Three nights later they returned to winning ways with a 2-0 triumph over AC Milan in Santa Clara before rounding off their stay in the States with a 2-1 defeat at the hands of AS Roma in St Louis.

Back on home soil and a reunion with ex-Reds Luis Suarez and Javier Mascherano awaited at Wembley. Almost 90,000 converged on the national stadium to witness this showpiece fixture and the majority went home happy as Liverpool handed out a 4-0 thrashing to the reigning La Liga champions.

Less than 24 hours later, and with a much-changed line-up, defeat by the same score away to Jürgen Klopp's former club FSV Mainz 05 brought pre-season to a close but the nine summer friendlies had more than served their purpose, with fitness levels honed, new signings settled and several youngsters blooded.

8 July – Tranmere Rovers (a) 1-0
13 July – Fleetwood Town (a) 5-0
17 July – Wigan Athletic (a) 2-0
20 July – Huddersfield Town (a) 2-0
28 July – Chelsea (Pasadena) 0-1
31 July – AC Milan (Santa Clara) 2-0
2 August – AS Roma (St Louis) 1-2
6 August – Barcelona (Wembley) 4-0
7 August – Mainz 05 (a) 0-4

PLAYER PROFILES

Kevin Stewart

Position: Midfield
Date of Birth: 7/9/1993
Birthplace: Enfield, England
Signed from: Tottenham Hotspur (July 2014)
Squad Number: 35

Danny Ings

Position: Forward
Date of Birth: 23/7/1992
Birthplace: Winchester, England
Signed from: Burnley (July 2015)
Squad Number: 28

Daniel Sturridge

Position: Forward
Date of Birth: 1/9/1989
Birthplace: Birmingham, England
Signed from: Chelsea (January 2013)
Squad Number: 15

Divock Origi

Position: Striker
Date of Birth: 18/4/1995
Birthplace: Ostend, Belgium
Signed from: Lille (July 2014)
Squad Number: 27

WE ARE THE FAMOUS, THE FAMOUS, KOPITES

Liverpudlians have long been renowned for their ingenuity when it comes to flag-making and it's debatable whether any other set of supporters can boast a collection as vast and varied as those that are regularly displayed on the Kop. As you can see, there's no need for plastic flags at Anfield...

Liddellpool - A respectful nod to the club's heritage, this flag pays tribute to the incomparable great of the 40s & 50s Billy Liddell

A banner made to honour the memory of young Liverpudlian Owen McVeigh, who sadly passed away during the 2015-16 season. Owen followed the Reds home and away, and regularly helped out with the flags on the Kop

A simple flag paying homage to the latest incumbent of the Anfield hot-seat and referencing one of his now famous soundbites

There are few finer sights in football than when the flags are out on the Kop ahead of another big European night at Anfield

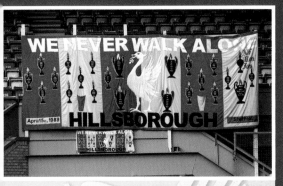

The brainchild of loyal Red and Hillsborough survivor Peter Carney, this flag was made to commemorate the 20th anniversary of the disaster and it features the names of all 96 victims

This giant flag has been a familiar sight at home games for a number of years and is ritually passed over the heads of Kopites before kick-off

We've Won It Five Times - a subtle reminder to those who may have forgotten that when it comes to British success in Europe, no one comes close to Liverpool Football Club

Men of Anfield - five of the club's managerial greats 'Shankly, Paisley, Fagan, Dalglish & Benitez' celebrated on the same banner

Win, lose or draw the loyalty of the Liverpool supporters is second to none

QUIZ AND PUZZLE ANSWERS

P20: GOAL!

P20: Name the Year

A. Charity Shield 1989
B. European Cup 1981
C. FA Cup 2006
D. League Cup 2003
E. Super Cup 2001

P21: Anagrams

LAGHDSIL - Dalglish   BLRAGOABRE - Grobbelaar

RGARDRE - Gerrard   NSLOAO - Alonso

SRNAEB - Barnes   ACMMNAMNA - McManaman

GENAKE - Keegan   YHAPYI - Hyypia

UZARES - Suarez   RGACHERAR - Carragher

P21: For Club & Country

Roberto Firmino – Brazil

Divock Origi – Belgium

Nathaniel Clyne – England

Georginio Wijnaldum – Holland

Emre Can – Germany

Sadio Mané – Senegal

Mamadou Sakho – France

Dejan Lovren – Croatia

P25: Spot the Difference

P31: Word Search

B	R	U	G	E	S	W	M	I	L	A	N	R	R	K	G
I	H	I	B	E	R	N	I	A	N	F	F	J	Y	W	L
N	H	N	K	T	V	V	G	A	C	I	F	N	E	B	R
T	O	W	W	T	A	Z	X	V	G	O	M	L	A	M	Y
E	N	Y	M	H	Y	U	L	M	X	O	C	G	G	F	Q
R	V	M	K	C	M	W	X	A	Q	E	C	R	T	N	Q
N	E	F	K	E	R	E	J	E	L	T	U	A	R	F	X
A	D	D	I	L	W	A	L	T	R	B	Q	N	N	N	G
Z	N	V	V	R	R	Q	I	L	S	R	H	O	Y	O	Z
I	C	A	A	E	B	C	J	G	I	A	E	L	H	Z	M
O	K	L	J	D	D	R	U	K	M	E	Y	E	N	B	W
N	P	E	K	N	T	A	O	B	N	W	S	C	M	Y	D
A	T	N	Y	A	F	B	U	N	A	Y	M	R	M	B	T
L	R	C	E	T	T	R	D	M	D	R	C	A	A	Z	Q
E	H	I	R	Y	G	T	O	V	J	B	R	B	M	M	C
X	X	A	Q	C	N	R	N	H	P	D	Y	M	M	N	X

P36: Dot-To-Dot

P46: Know Your Team

1. Red Star Belgrade
2. Four
3. Roberto Firmino
4. Loris Karius
5. Norwich City
6. Emre Can
7. Joe Allen
8. Philippe Coutinho
9. St Mary's Stadium
10. Adam Lallana
11. Joel Matip
12. Coventry City
13. 2007
14. Daniel Sturridge
15. Danny Ward

P47: Fill in the missing blanks

Prior to signing for Liverpool James Milner played for Leeds, Newcastle United, **Aston Villa**, and Manchester City.

Liverpool fielded five debutants in the FA Cup third round tie at Exeter last season – Sheyi Ojo, Kevin Stewart, Tiago Ilori, Ryan Kent and **Joe Maguire**.

During Liverpool's run to the 2016 Europa League final they defeated Augsburg, Manchester United, **Borussia Dortmund** and Villarreal in the knockout rounds.

P47: Odd One Out

Which club have Liverpool not met in a European final –
(Atletico Madrid)

Who was Liverpool's only representative at the 2016 Copa America –
(Philippe Coutinho)

In which country did Liverpool not play Europa League fixture in 2015/16 –
(Italy)

P46: True or False?

Daniel Sturridge started his career with Manchester City

> **TRUE**

Jon Flanagan was a boyhood Evertonian

> **FALSE**

Jürgen Klopp once played for Bayern Munich

> **FALSE**

Anfield has a bigger capacity than the Parc de Prince in Paris

> **TRUE**

P52: Spot the Ball

P47: Penalty Prize

Luis Suarez v Sunderland (h) Premier League, 13 August 2011 – **Missed**

Mario Balotelli v Besiktas (h) Europa League round of 32, 19 February 2015 – **Scored**

Steven Gerrard v Queens Park Rangers (h) Premier League, 2 May 2015 – **Missed**

Daniel Sturridge v Manchester United (h) Europa League round of 16, 10 March 2016 – **Scored**

Christian Benteke v Crystal Palace (a) Premier League, 16 March 2016 – **Scored**

WHERE'S MIGHTY RED?